The Millionaire Recruiter

Get Rich with No Experience

Brianna Rooney
Owner and Founder of
Techees

ISBN-10: 1983746053
ISBN-13: 978-1983746055

Cover Design: Emily Stellick

Editing: Rachel Uphill

Printed in the USA

Table of Contents

Preface

Hello there!
Congratulations on picking up this book. For those that don't know what you are about to read, I'll give you a quick rundown. This is an introduction into the world of recruiting (AKA headhunting), how you can make a successful career out of it and a sh*t ton of money.

Who am I?
Brianna Rooney, at your service. I'm the Founder of Techees Recruiting (techees.com) and the World's Best Wingman (I'll explain the second part later). I've been in the recruiting industry for over a decade and started out with absolutely no knowledge about recruiting. I worked really hard as an employee for two years, earning north of $150,000 per year as a 21 year old and coming straight out of a bartending job. I then used my experience to open up my own recruiting business that has been successfully running ever since.

Why are you here?
Hopefully, because you want to be a millionaire! You picked this book up because you're ready to better yourself, your life and your future. You're here to discover a new career that will take you further than your wildest dreams. Perhaps you are a bit lost, a new grad or just someone looking for a better living.

No matter your situation, it's all good news. There are no 'buts' or 'what ifs' or pre-requisites for reading this. The book will show you how any person from any background can be a success. It's very possible to make a ton of money within your first year as a recruiter. I only ask you to believe in yourself. You're here reading because you want to gain financial success and you believe that it's possible. All that is required is a strong passion, focus, and willingness to work hard.

Ready?
If you have no idea what recruiting is, don't worry. This book will give you a complete overview of the industry. I'm going to go over how you'll earn huge paychecks by following the steps I teach. Once you are done and get a feel for how this works, you'll be ready to start my eCourse and be on your way to dominating a powerful and lucrative industry.

Okay, let's jump in!

PART 1

How I became a recruiter and why you should, too (hint, hint: for the money)

My story: How I became a recruiter

I've always loved matchmaking. And I'm good at it. Some people have a knack for putting two people together for love and I have that knack too... but not just for love – for success. Business success, career success. I'm Brianna Rooney. I'm a tech recruiter and I love it.

I actually stumbled my way into this industry. I had only just heard of it when I started but fate and hard work came together as my perfect match. And it can for you, too.

I don't believe you're reading this by accident. This is YOUR fate moment. And **I can teach you how to do what I do - and go from just learning about it to making over $100,000 a year**. The following is a bit about me and my journey, maybe it will be similar to yours in a few short months...

At 20 years old, I was a fresh graduate of The Fashion Institute of Design and Merchandising (FIDM). I was eager to invest my talents in having my own store until harsh reality hit. I'd need money – a lot of money. Talent alone wasn't going to get me my store.

So I set out on a path to make money by matchmaking again – this time with my own life. I brought together two of my favorite things: money and partying. I attended bartending school and for the next two years, I had one of the best times of my life. But time was only passing and all I had was a whole lot of boozy stories and not nearly enough money saved. I knew it was time for a real job. One that didn't require me to take a taxi home because I'd had too much fun.

I met up with a friend one night at BJ's for some drinks and career advice. She was a recruiter for the accounting industry and thought that my personality was perfect for recruiting. I was floored that I could actually get paid to be a type of matchmaker – a career matchmaker. Someone who fills positions in companies with the perfect fit. I decided then and there that I was going to research everything I could about the field as soon as I got home. Yet the universe was already one step ahead of me. Before dinner was even over, my phone rang. It was fate calling.

Fate was a recruiter who'd seen my resume on Monster.com. He asked if I'd ever heard of recruiting. I was instantly convinced that this was, indeed, my destiny and perhaps my true calling. I agreed to an interview.

At the interview the next day, the recruiting firm owner went on and on about how much money I could make placing software engineers for startup companies in the Bay Area. Of course, he had me at "money" but then asked me a question I'll never forget: How much money did I want to make? "Hmmm," I thought, "is this a trick question?" Figuring I had nothing to lose at 22 years old and with no experience, I blurted out, "$300k". He hired me on the spot.

I was crazy excited. I called my parents and told them I was going to be rich. Instead of being thrilled, they warned me to be careful because it must be a scam. I went through with it anyway and made almost $90k my first year and each year afterward I made significantly more.

I was making amazing money and loving what I was doing but, after two years of working for that recruiting company, I knew I could be doing things much better than I was trained to do. The industry requires a lot of connections, referrals, and repeat business to make the perfect matches. So why wasn't I trained to operate in that way? I decided that to be truly successful and to handle each position with the care and finesse required, it needed to be that way. So with guts, a loose plan, some self-training (with a bit of trial and error), and a credit card, I successfully ventured out on my own.

Today I own Techees, two homes, and a restaurant. I have a wonderful husband who's a chef and two beautiful children. But it didn't happen by accident. Yes, fate definitely played a part – but hard work and hustle made it happen.

There is a science to recruiting and a code to live and do business by. This job changes people's lives every day and it should not be taken lightly. It transformed my life. If you want it to, it can transform your life, too. And I can get you there.

As I grew Techees to be the best in my industry I was becoming sought after to help train others while I was training my own employees. I wanted to reach more individuals and teach them how to become successful, so I decided to put my secrets into a full-fledged eCourse. If you like what you hear by the end of this book, I encourage you to sign up. You'll gain a whole world of inside knowledge and a step-by-step guide to find massive success in recruiting.

I guarantee my eCourse is not just theory, it is full of real help and solid guidance. I love recruiting and I continue to recruit every day. I stay in the thick of the pulse and changes in the industry. Everything you'll learn from me will bring you the success I've had – and perhaps even greater success.

So if what you've read has ignited your imagination to all the possibilities, I'm here to guide you every step of the way. Let's get working so you can accomplish more than you ever thought possible, faster than you ever thought possible!

Let's Talk About Money and Why You Want it

Money is an interesting beast. It's at the core of all our problems and successes yet, society tells us it's taboo to talk about. If your desire for wanting more money makes people around you uncomfortable then kick them to the curb. It only sounds greedy to people who know they won't be successful themselves. Those are the ones who will hold you back from reaching your potential. Surround yourself with other successful people and those who want to be successful like you. You'll find that openly talking about money and how to get it is refreshingly honest and real when it's with like-minded people.

I'm an open book with my family and friends and I think that is a key factor in being successful. I love money and I'm driven towards it. I believe those who say they don't want or need money are the ones who have convinced themselves they won't ever be rich. They've given up the possibility of being super successful because they've decided it's too much work or they aren't one of the lucky ones. It doesn't matter what age they are either.

So get rid of the thoughts in your head and the peoplewho tell you it's okay not to be rich. I want to help you change that. And I can. I've changed it

for myself, for numerous others, and I can change it for you. You don't have to try to convince yourself that money isn't important anymore.

As we go along, I'll share more about myself and my experience. **I believe being real and honest is one of the keys to success.** You don't need to tell people the reason you want to be rich is so you can help solve world hunger or save the dolphins. Seriously, be honest! Make a list right now and write down why you want to be successful. It doesn't matter how selfish or vain your reasons are. Do you just love the idea of being rich? The financial freedom it gives? Do you want to retire early? Own a big house or luxury cars? Travel the world? Have bragging rights over your friends? Give to the causes you believe in? Give back to your family who has loved and supported you? **Just last year I bought my 90 year old Grandma her dream car: a bright red Mini Cooper. Talk about being the favorite grandchild.**

Whatever your reason, it doesn't matter. What does matter is that you have your why crystal clear and written down. **Then keep this list close to remind you WHY you want, or rather NEED, to be successful. These reasons are what will drive you to hustle and work your butt off to get there.**
Facebook: @millionairerecruiter   11

How I Found My "Why"

Your why is what drives you. Master that – and you'll master everything. So with that in mind, here is a bit about where my "why" originated.

I'm not shy to admit that from a very young age, I wanted to have money and lots of it. My parents got divorced when I was 10 and I saw firsthand what having money – or should I say, what having no money – does. Let me be clear, I am not going to say I was sad about my parents getting divorced, or that I was scarred by it. I am thrilled my parents got divorced when they did because that helped make me into the successful person I am today. I believe no one should settle in life.

After the divorce announcement, my mom moved my brother and me down the street to live in a condo together. We loved it! We had a tennis court, a pool and, best of all, a happy mom. However, just a few short months later, the three of us had to move back in with dad. It wasn't that I didn't want to live with my dad. I had a great relationship with him and enjoyed seeing him more, but that was not the point. It wasn't because my parents were getting back together. We had to move back because she couldn't afford to live on her own. Even though my mom worked very hard and often very late, it still wasn't enough.

I knew from that day on I would never let myself be in that situation. I wanted to be able to make my own decisions and have choices. I didn't want to be forced to go down a path because I had no choice. And I've kept that promise to myself.

I've forged my own path in the world of tech recruiting and have the success and money I promised myself I'd have. From that success I now get asked all the time:
- How do you do this?
- What is recruiting?
- Why do you get paid so well?
- How long will it take to start making money?
  How much money can someone make?
- Do I need a degree?
- Do you think I can be a recruiter?

I'm going to answer these questions for you in this book but let's get two out of the way right now: **No! You do NOT need a degree. And YES! You CAN be a successful recruiter. I'll show you how.**

Desiring Money Fuels Your Drive

As you get to know me, and I coach you, you'll **see more and more of my passion and fire and drive.** These go hand-in-hand with knowing your why. I believe **we all have passion and fire and drive and we all have a personal why. You just need to discover them and learn to harness them** so you, too, can become very, very rich.

Being rich may be a big part of fueling your drive. It is for me. Now, **some people take offense at the desire to be rich and successful but I look at it differently. Money is a *tool* to be used for good.** Not just for yourself but for others.

Let's be real for a moment: You cannot honestly look at yourself in the mirror when your bank account is $5k or less and think, "Yeah, I'm okay with this. I want for nothing." Even if you are personally okay with not exploring the world of travel, going to plays and musicals, trying restaurants, etc. You're lying to yourself to say you also don't care to help anyone in need. That it doesn't matter to you that a child goes hungry or an elderly person with dementia has no money for care. **As selfish as we can sometimes be as human beings, we all care about others.**

What I'm saying is that **money doesn't have to be used for "things"**. **You can be rich without being spoiled and self-indulgent. Money can be used for countless good acts**. Yet, you'll never be able to do much good if you settle for just scraping by. **You cannot give what you don't have.** And you never know how much good you can do if you don't push **yourself to your full potential. Everyone has more drive inside them then they realize.**

Let me share with you my personal experience to illustrate my above point about drive. I was four years into my own business, Techees, and I was content. I was happy making $250k+ a year. Yet, I caught myself slipping. I wasn't working nearly as hard as I did when I first started. It happened gradually, and because I was making more money, I hadn't noticed. It took me having my first child to realize I'd let my fire die down.

When Diego arrived, I now had more to live for, plus more expenses. And any time spent away from my little boy was too precious to waste. I knew I had to push my limits. That year, I worked almost 4 ½ months less than everyone in my office of 10 and yet closed more deals than all of them. **Yes – 4 ½ months worth of LESS work time – and I closed more deals**. The resulting mixed emotions rekindled my fire. I was half disappointed in myself and half proud of myself. I realized that I'd always been capable of this amount of production.

Shame on me for finding that out 6 years into my career as a recruiter! On the other hand, I was very proud that I'd hit another level of success and a whole new tier of money I once didn't think plausible. **I'd discovered the true magic of drive.**

I share that illustration because I know from personal experience it is possible to push for more. **I continue to push the limits of how much money I can make.** And it doesn't just start and stop with the money – the fire and passion I have for recruiting is also personally fulfilling. **You, too, can push the limits on how much money you can make so you can do good in this world. AND you can have a career that is truly personally fulfilling! That is the magic of drive.**

PART 2

An introduction to recruiting

Just what *is* recruiting?

It's interesting. I've been doing this for over 10 years, and I still get this question all the time. For you, it's the perfect starter question because **it's natural to think: "Wait. How is this an actual job? Don't companies just post positions and people apply and HR does the rest?"** One day, you'll chuckle at these questions along with me because, frankly, it's much, much more intricate than that.

Let me lay it out simply to start. I was confused myself when I first heard of the recruiting industry, so I've been on both sides.

Companies need help with hiring talent. This is because the really talented people are nearly always already employed. The ones actively looking for positions tend to be those that are looking due to a specific life change. They may have been laid off or even fired.

The bottom line is – companies want the people they can't have. They want the ones that are already performing. The superstars. That's human nature. As I mentioned in my story, this job is extremely similar to being a matchmaker. As we work together, you'll see how similar interviewing and hiring is to dating. That's why I call myself "the world's best wingman". But it pays so much more than matching up dates.

Companies pay big money to have a recruiter match them up with the perfect new employee.

Here's a quick definition that might help:

> *Recruiter/Headhunter: An individual hired by a corporation to locate a suitable candidate with a certain skill set. The skill set is often harder to find or requires a certain background, necessitating the use of a recruiter.*

You may be surprised to learn that every industry uses recruiters. Tech recruiting just happens to be an industry that has a very high demand and a lot of competition. Software engineering for the Bay Area (Silicon Valley) in California is always in need.

Let me ease your mind right now: **You DO NOT need to know anything about the actual work done in the field you recruit for. What I mean is that you do not need to be a software engineer to recruit one.** You will learn some of the lingo, and that helps, but you do not need to actually know how to engineer software.

"The secret of my success is that we have gone to exceptional lengths to hire the best people in the world. Recruiting is hard. It's just finding the needles in the haystack." – Steve Jobs

Outsiders might view this job as easy and not needed. They could not be more wrong. **If recruiters weren't needed, why would companies pay a $20k-$40k referral fee for each person placed? Or upwards of $40k-$100k per placement of executives** such as CTOs, CIOs, CMOS, CFOs, and CEOs? **They wouldn't.**

The truth is, hiring the right people takes a lot of time and effort. **We free up time for companies to do what they do best, which is to build their product and get it out.** Not spend hours upon hours searching for possible candidates and interviewing. They do what they do best while hiring recruiters to do what we do best. **We find the people that can build their product, build it the best, and build it the fastest.**

I get resumes in front of the person that actually makes the hiring decisions. This benefits both the proper candidate AND the company. Because, frankly, someone can be the most talented candidate, but companies get hundreds of resumes a day. Most are not qualified. Having a huge number of resumes to dig through, isn't feasible. The fact that only 10% of applicants are relevant makes this a daunting and low-priority task for companies. They don't have those hours to spare. So **even great candidates are just sending their resumes to a black hole of death trying to apply by themselves. I am their sunshine.** I often make a candidates' dream come true.

There is nothing more personal to someone than their family and friends and their career. Some might say their career is the most important thing in their life. **The ability to get someone a job that changes their life and their family's lives is the most amazing feeling. Not to mention getting paid really, really well to do it.** That's a definite win-win!

A simplified example of how recruiting works

Remember how I said that **you do not need to actually know how everything works in the field you're recruiting**? In other words, you do not need to know how to engineer software to recruit a software engineer. **What you actually need to know is how to match the right person with the right position**. Again, it's like matchmaking – but for careers. And **this is precisely what my eCourse will teach you.**

To give you a simplified example to start, think of it this way: what you'll actually get extremely good at is keyword searches and matching everything together with a resume and personality. **Companies tell you exactly who (what skills) they need; you become the matchmaker.**

Just how does that work? First of all, you technically work for the company offering the position because that's who will pay you for a successful placement. However, without a candidate to give them, you would never make any money. I teach you how to have BOTH contacts.

Here's an example client scenario:

Facebook needs a software engineer with x,y, and z experience. They will go into great detail as to who they are looking for, sometimes even down to which schools the person should have attended, and the personality type they prefer.

Now that you have all the requirements, you then go on Linkedin. I teach you in detail in my eCourse precisely how to use this source to find someone that matches those requirements.

Now you must quickly develop a relationship with your potential candidate out of nothing. This in itself is a skill I help you develop all throughout my eCourse – because, let's face it, without being at least somewhat of a "people person" you won't go too far in anything in life. At bare minimum, you need to at least have an illusion of being a people person, that is, know how to interact with people in a way they will respond to positively.

As you get to know your potential candidate, you're learning about them and feeling out if they are a good fit for the open position. They, in turn, are deciding if it is a fit for them as well. Sometimes you will help at least a little bit to persuade them. Once you both feel it is a fit, you send their resume over to your contact at Facebook.

(Of course, you will give Facebook a few candidates to consider, increasing your chances of finding their perfect match.)

Since you're so well trained by my eCourse, the hiring manager will want to talk to this person. At that point, you'll be setting up this person's interviews. There are typically 1-2 phone interviews, followed by an onsite interview lasting about 2-4 hours. After that, within 24-48 hours Facebook, hopefully, gets back to you with a "Yes".

This is where the real fun begins. You have an offer! This is the most exciting part of recruiting! Well, besides cashing your checks, of course. Presenting an offer, negotiating, and closing a deal are the final steps in the candidate's interview process and the last step before you get paid.

I **cannot stress enough how important it is to know how to negotiate.** You will need to be able to make both the company and candidate feel like they're getting the best deal. If you know how and when to negotiate, you will remain in control through the process and have a higher success rate.

Because it's so important, there is a whole chapter dedicated to this in my eCourse. You will be involved in negotiating your candidate's offer but **don't let this intimidate you. You will become the ultimate negotiator with the skills I will teach you.** Just like learning to be a people person, negotiating is something that will help you throughout your entire life, so learning this skill can help you outside this career as well.

When it comes to the offer, companies handle it in all different ways. Some present it themselves, ask you for suggestions, and keep you in the loop. Some just present it and don't consult you (which I think is an idiotic way of doing it). And others rely on you to tell them what to do and you present it (my favorite).

In a perfect world, your candidate accepts a good offer, puts in their two-week notice, starts at Facebook, and is happy there for years. Of course, the negotiation process is often more complex than that but, again, I'll teach you what you need to know.

Once your candidate starts at Facebook, **you send Facebook a hefty (but well deserved) bill of 20% of this person's salary.** I go into fee agreements in great detail in my eCourse so you know how to negotiate, you know what's normal (also known as "industry standard") and know what you can't compromise on.

Facebook is happy, and your candidate is happy. Now your candidate writes a glowing recommendation of you on Linkedin, and whenever the time comes to look again for a different position, they will, of course, reach back out to you. I have to say that not much is better than placing someone multiple times. I'm still looking for my 4th placement for the same candidate. Meaning, I've placed a couple people at three different companies over the years but I've yet to see someone placed four times. It will happen – I know it!

I hope you're doing **the math in your head as to how lucrative this can be** and how quickly you can move up in the recruiting world. Recruiting is a giant industry that no one knows much about, but everyone needs it. It's **the best-kept secret – and you're invited into the inner circle.**

Internal versus External Recruiting

Let me be right up front and say: I endorse being an external recruiter. I'm an external recruiter. I have been an external recruiter for over ten years. I love it! Would I ever switch to internal? Not a chance in hell. Why? I was able to make a whole pile of money at my first job at an external recruiting firm. After I learned the ins and outs and how the formula worked, I was able to leave and start my own external recruiting agency. I grew it to fifteen employees who all recruit and make money for me.

I'm not saying internal recruiting is a bad way to go but it does look and pay differently. And I assume you're reading this book because you're looking for a job that has no limits on how much money you can make. You want a non-conventional, play by your own rules job, you want to hustle, and you want to set your hours.

That said, **let me break down the main differences between being an internal versus external recruiter**, and you'll quickly see why I encourage you to choose to become an external.

Internal recruiting: You work for one company like you would at any other typical job. Your job is to hire people to work at that specific company. Basically, it's a position within HR. You review resumes, interview potential candidates, and are responsible to fill positions.

And guess what? If you don't fill those vacancies, it's your ass on the line. You're in a salaried position and it's just expected that you'll do your job. If you struggle to find someone as quickly as the company demands, you could be in trouble. And even if you do a great job, you aren't likely to get much more than a pat on the back – or maybe (if you're lucky) a small $5000 bonus for filling a tough position.

All that hard work, and it's still a long climb to the top, with only a salary increase maybe once a year. If they don't freeze wages, that is.

External recruiting: You work at a recruiting agency which contracts with a multiple of companies to fill a variety of positions they have open. Your job is to fill positions at those companies, but you technically don't work for them as their employee.

As an external recruiter, you control the hours you work and how much money you can make. You work on commission so more deals = more money.

When you work for an agency, a percentage of any deal goes to the firm and you keep the rest. The firm/agency takes a cut of the deal and in exchange they provide you with resources, such as leads, to set you up for success.

In addition to getting commission for making a deal, as an external recruiter, **you can even make double money by representing *both* sides in a deal** – both the company hiring AND the candidate they choose to hire. That's like hitting a grand slam!

What's the biggest difference between working as an internal recruiter versus an external recruiter? An external recruiter works on commission. When you work on commission, you control your financial destiny. And you can make a whole lot more money.

I get that it can be scary at first to go to a commission-based position. It's risky to leave a steady paycheck and venture out. But you won't be stuck on a salary grinding away for that small promotion. **You get to reap the benefits of your own work instead of working to satisfy the needs of your company.**

You'll be shocked at how much working on commission lights a fire under you. **You get to grind and claw your way to more deals and bigger paychecks.** In a recruiting agency, everyone has one goal: close as many deals and make as much money as possible.

I promise, even though it's scary at first, once you hit your stride and make it over the hump in the recruiting world, your earnings potential flies through the roof. You'll know if you can handle working on commission within 3-6 months. If you can survive that, you can do it permanently.

And again, **I presume you're here because you want to live an exciting lifestyle with no cash limits!** You can't do that stuck in a cubicle on a measly salary. **To make big-time money, you have to take risks.** I'll be with you every step of the way when you take my eCourse. I'll teach you step-by-step everything you need to know to become a recruiting expert.

Part 3

Recruiting is your ticket to the life you've always wanted

Why commission-based jobs beat the sh*t out of salary positions

It's been over 10 years since I've had a "normal" job. You're taught in school and by your parents, and it's reinforced by society in general, that you need to work hard and follow orders. You're supposed to put in extra hours to get noticed by the boss. You'll get promoted over the course of several years, as you earn it, and you work toward the hope of making it into management. That's why **I strongly dislike salaried positions**.

All the while you're busting your ass you're not getting paid for all that overtime and sacrifices you're making. Salary employees don't get overtime because they have "job security" and benefits. You work like a dog in hopes of a favorable annual review where you pray to get a 5-10% raise (and 10% would be on the high side). It's a very long grind to hit $100k+.

On the other hand, if you have a commission-based job and bust your ass, it shows in your bank account.

Let's look at this with a "best case" salary scenario...

Let's say you're 21, you get a salary cubicle job (what fun) – and you're started at $36,000 (which would already be a high salary).

You work your ass off every year putting in 50-60 hours a week, waiting hand and foot on your boss and manager. You're the star employee so each year they give you the highest raise they can afford (5%). You appreciate it and feel you really deserve more after all your dedication but that's the company cap. Now let's take a look at the next 15 years of income for your years of dedication...

Year	Increase 5%	Salary
1	x	$ 36,000.00
2	$ 1,800.00	$ 37,800.00
3	$ 1,890.00	$ 39,690.00
4	$ 1,984.50	$ 41,674.50
5	$ 2,083.73	$ 43,758.23
6	$ 2,187.91	$ 45,946.14
7	$ 2,297.31	$ 48,243.44
8	$ 2,412.17	$ 50,655.62
9	$ 2,532.78	$ 53,188.40
10	$ 2,659.42	$ 55,847.82
11	$ 2,792.39	$ 58,640.21
12	$ 2,932.01	$ 61,572.22
13	$ 3,078.61	$ 64,650.83
14	$ 3,232.54	$ 67,883.37
15	$ 3,394.17	$ 71,277.54

Now, you might be saying, "Hey, making over double by the time I'm in my mid-30s – and I'd be making way more than the U.S. average at that age. Doesn't sound too bad!" **But wait, Super Star, not only have you not even hit 6 figures – you've not paid for anything yet.**

You've not paid anything in taxes. You've not paid for insurances or saved for retirement. You've not even bought food or have a place to live.

Sometime over those 15 years, you're likely to want a house. People don't want to pay rent forever. But a down payment on a $200,000 house (which is close to the average price in the U.S.) would be $40,000, not including all the other closing costs, moving expenses, etc. That's more than you're bringing home in a year for the first half of your 15 years.

And what if you want to get married? Have children? Then you better hope your spouse or significant other makes just as much, if not more, than you. Seriously! Don't get me started on how much kids cost.

The point is, I'd imagine your $70,000 salary after 15 long years isn't looking so great right now. It's being cut into small pieces and you're not sure how much is even going to be left over.

Not to mention the fact that you're definitely not working less. Each year your salary grew, so did the size and scope of your work, how much time you have to put in, and your company responsibilities. And **all this is based on you landing an above average opportunity in the first place! In order to have more, you have to take on a second job or a side hustle.**

So now that you've faced financial reality, let me ask you this: **What DO you want?** Do you want to save and save and save just to hope you can retire at age 65? Do you want to pinch every penny just to go on vacation every other year? Or **do you want better?**

If you want better – and I suspect you do – I invite you to do what I did. **Grow a pair of brass balls and take some risks.** Not a day goes by where I regret the struggles I've had (and still have) working on commission because the success outweighs it all by a long shot.

Personally, every year I've done significantly better than the last. While you're celebrating $61k a year at age 32, I celebrated over 6 times that amount every year for the past 5 years – all while working 32 hours a week. **I want you to have my kind of success to celebrate.**

In recruiting, you make commission off every candidate you place.

Your bank account is rewarded significantly for every accomplishment, not a small reward for the accumulation of an entire year of accomplishments.

The **only person standing in your way to YOUR better - is you. You control what you make. You design your destiny.** I'm not going to act like it's all rainbows and unicorns; it's a real job, it's hard work, you have to put in the time. But the beauty of recruiting is that it's a relationship building job. The more you build, the more referrals you get. That never goes away. The better the work you do, the more you get recognized. So it does get smoother over time. You just have to begin. Don't stand in your own way.

Discredit the "you'll only succeed by working yourself to the bone" myth

There is a common concept that working longer hours = making more money. That's true when you're working in the trade of hours for dollars, such as earning an hourly wage. Then yes, obviously the more you work, the more you make. Of course, that isn't the case at all with salaried positions. And not even close with commission-based work. I talk more about the differences in what you can make later on in this book. Suffice to say right now, **there is no need to overexert yourself in recruiting if you're putting in the *right* effort.** Remember how I realized I'd worked 4 ½ months LESS in time than others but landed more deals? It's not only possible – it's reality. **You don't need to work like a dog to succeed. Not in recruiting.**

Let me clarify what I mean by "working like a dog". **You will work hard and hustle. But you don't need to work full time to earn $150,000+ a year.** My employees and I work 32 hours per week and often find time to celebrate accomplishments with weekly boozy team lunches, mansion weekends in Big Bear, shopping sprees in Beverly Hills, massages at The Four Seasons, etc. We enjoy the fruits of our labor without wearing ourselves down. I have a family to attend to and own a restaurant.

I don't have time to work late into the night and definitely not on weekends. And I don't need to. Neither do you.

In a strange twist of reality, I've actually seen the *worst* performing recruiters be the ones to put in the *most* hours. The reason is simple. They have fallen for the myth that working more automatically means better performance. They haven't figured it out. **When you learn to work efficiently and are self-disciplined, you'll max out your commissions without having to work 60 hour weeks.** You don't have to put in long hours every night just to impress your boss. You don't have to give up your weekends. And you certainly don't have to burn yourself out.

How? I've learned how to budget my time and hone my skills by using what's available to me. I don't waste any energy or effort when it comes to my work. I'll teach you how to approach this job the way I do.

The best way to become a successful recruiter is to use the resources around you. There is an abundance of tools and outlets that others simply don't use or pay attention to. **I go over all of these in my eCourse and show you how to use them effectively.**

Along with those, pay attention to your surroundings. Learn from your own pitfalls, as well as the mistakes of peers.

You don't have to reinvent in the wheel, just do better than the person next to you. Constantly adapt and refine your approach. **I'm a believer that the *smarter* and more *efficiently* you work, the bigger the payouts.**

So how *do* you get enough done in the day? How do you know if you're putting in the right amount of work? **Start by making it your mission to determine that threshold where efficient work deteriorates into fruitless or mindless busy work.**

Here's an example scenario for how you do that:

You find that an average of 75 emails sent that day resulted in 15 responses.

You reflect on your day and realize you spent one hour scrolling through your email or browsing Linkedin – neither of which actually was fruitful.

You realize you could have spent that time more efficiently and sent out 20 more emails instead. You might have received 4-5 more responses.

One of those responses could have been the lead to your next deal and big commission check.

Now you've identified what your new threshold is. The next day you send 95 emails to achieve maximum efficiency. You've adapted and reworked your approach.

Now, of course, you don't want this to spiral into just sending more and more emails. That's not the point. **The point is that you've replaced an unprofitable hour with one that is profitable.**

Secondly, prioritize your day. Figure out what's most important for each day. What needs to be completed now? What can you save for later? Learning which tasks will result in making a deal is an integral part of the job.

Prioritizing is not hard but focus can be. **You'll learn how to focus on what is important and set aside what isn't.** That discipline of focus and executing day in and day out is the difference between successful recruiters and ones that just get by. You'll become a well-oiled machine.

Finally, just because you're not working on weekends or burning the midnight oil doesn't mean that the work is easy. I don't want you to get the wrong impression. Cutting big commission checks will never be easy.

It's going to take a lot of hard work, I repeat, hard work - but efficient and smart work, nonetheless. **Once you learn how to work hard the *right* way, you'll work hard but it won't require full time.**

Nearly anyone can learn to be a "people person"

Of course, some personality types are those excluded by the "nearly" in the above statement. Honestly, though, if you're reading this, you're likely not one of those I'd exclude. You CAN learn to be a "people person" – or at least know how to talk to people in a way that will yield a positive response – even if you've never been one before.

Recruiting is a wonderful platform to develop those skills AND get paid in the process! Recruiting can help you reinvent yourself.

Let me give you an example by sharing a bit about one of my employees...

He came from a cubicle job at an insurance company making a steady, but measly, $34k a year. He took a chance and quit that job, jumping into the unknown. He barely knew anything about the world of recruiting and he took the job on commission, not knowing when his next paycheck could come. Why would he do that? Because he knew that he could do better than earning $136 a day before taxes.

The thought of the risk excited him. The motivation sparked something inside him.

He knew he was capable, and with the right training and focus, he could make life-changing money. And he did. In his second year, he made $105k – making $45k in commission one of the months. After he **realized he made $11k MORE in ONE month than he did in a whole year at his previous job**, he knew he made the right decision.

To get there, this employee **transformed into a people person**. He became a fearless baller on the phone that could handle any type of client call. He went into a completely new career path and started over from scratch. You can, too.

With my eCourse, you can become an expert within a year. You don't have to have a degree or even any prior experience. You just have to be willing to hustle and put yourself out there. You have to be unwilling to settle. There is so much more opportunity out there in the world. **You don't have to set your expectations low just because you don't have professional work experience or don't know any better.**

Recruiting is like sales in that you have to constantly be hustling and selling yourself. Be bold. Part of what goes into that hustle is talking to both clients and job seekers that are asking for your help, so you will have to step out of your comfort zone. But I promise that putting yourself out there gets easier the more you do it.

It also adds exponentially to your success in life. **People who are willing to do things that make them uncomfortable are the most successful in life**. Opening yourself up to new experiences and being willing to learn molds you into a well-rounded and wiser person. That, and remembering that facing criticism and embarrassing yourself is simply part of the process. To say that I've never had an embarrassing moment would be a terrible lie - it happens to everyone! Don't fret and don't worry about what other people think. I know that the more risks I take the more money I'll earn. Keep that in mind.

Beyond that, networking and building relationships is a skill for life. The "self-made millionaire" doesn't actually exist. No one ever gets rich completely on their own. They always seek help, find mentors, and learn from their peers.

As scary as it sounds, the best way to start building those personal skills is by jumping right into cold emailing and calling. It's by far one of the best experiences you can have to face the professional world. Anyone will tell you that cold calling has only benefitted them. It's a great way to grow thick skin and not let getting rejected phase you. Bottom line is, getting rejected is part of the job. It happens more often than not and those who can stomach it are the ones that last in this industry.

Cold emailing and calling will also teach you how to quickly build a rapport with the person on the other end of the line. You'll find that the more you do it, the more comfortable you will be talking to strangers. Your conversations will slowly start to get longer. The nerves will die down. You'll understand how to engage people more and personalize the subject matter.

The beauty is that this will naturally roll over into being able to network in person and strike up conversations with anyone you meet. You'll be able to read people and match their tone. You'll understand what people want to hear and you'll know what questions to ask. It becomes ingrained in you and you'll see it turn into a positive personality trait.

With the help of my eCourse, you will evolve and transform through each and every experience. As you develop relationships and get more contracts, you will morph into a people person. Better yet, your commission checks will get bigger and bigger!

The importance of standing out in the recruiting world

Recruiters don't always have the best reputation – which is great for you because it's so easy to be good and set yourself apart. Being a recruiter is one of the best and most lucrative jobs in the world. You can go from zero to hero in 2.5 seconds.

However, recruiting does require both an extreme passion to be the best and a hyper-focused work ethic. It's imperative to stand out and go the extra mile. Those recruiters that set themselves apart from the rest are far more successful. I'll show you in greater detail how to be creative and unique in my eCourse.

I think you're ready to stand out because you've stuck with me thus far through this book. And the good news is that you don't have to have any kind of professional knowledge or experience or even a degree to stand out. That's right, you can be just as successful as someone who comes in with a fancy degree. You just have to have the drive and be coachable.

I'll share a bit about my own experience with this to prove my point about not needing a fancy degree…

When I started in recruiting, I didn't have any relevant sales experience and I didn't have a degree in business or anything related. I'd graduated from The Fashion Institute of Design and Merchandising (FIDM), remember?

The day I started happened to be on the same day as another girl. She'd gotten her business degree from a top school in California *and* she had prior sales experience from Enterprise Rent-A-Car.

At that recruiting agency, there were two teams. My boss let the manager choose if he wanted me (no experience, no relevant degree) or this other person with a business degree and sales experience. Well, of course, he definitely wasn't choosing me. But I ended up happy he didn't.

That rejection ignited my fire and I closed three deals my very first month. Something that agency had never seen before. The other person didn't have her first deal until 4 months later and was let go 9 months after that. Getting picked last and not having the "perfect on paper" qualifications didn't feel so bad anymore because it drove me to prove myself.

I stood out and continued to stand out because I refused to let my lack of experience or a relevant degree define my success. **The key is being trained properly and applying that training well.**

Part of that training includes how to stand out in recruiting. And one way to do that is to never waste a client's time. I'll show you how to work efficiently so you're not spending extra hours and putting in time on projects that won't make you money fast and won't get you quality referrals. With proper training, you won't be wasting your time or anyone else's.

Speaking of referrals, referrals are key. You'll notice the better recruiters have significantly more recommendations on their Linkedin profiles. Once you get referrals, business will come to you because you stand out.

And **when you stand out – you land deals. When you land deals, you make money. When you make money, you're happy. Plain and simple.**

Part 4

Take action and control your future!

Take Action and control your future!

You made it to the end...which is really just the beginning. Now you have a choice. It's time to take action and control your future! It's time to stop leaving your future up to the typical path that so many people take.

The recruiting business will give you as much as you give it. There are countless job openings across the United States in all industries. In fact, a report released April of 2017 gave a record high stat: 6 million job openings! Just think: **If you could just place 1% of that**, it would be over 66,000 placements. The average placement is $28,000. Did you get out your calculator? I did when I read that report and nearly had a heart attack. **It comes to $1.85 BILLION dollars.** I officially have the money chills!

Don't just *tell* yourself you're going to do this. GO DO IT! It doesn't matter what you went to college for or if you even went at all. It doesn't matter if you're not an outgoing person or if you don't know your way around a computer. I used to type with my two pointer fingers! **All you need is a positive attitude, a willingness to learn, and a spirit that is motivated to work hard.** I'm not just talking about you wanting money or needing money. I'm talking about **what makes you tick – what drives you to make money – a lot of it. The rest you can learn.**

Challenge yourself every day. Never be satisfied. Keep going. Make monthly goals, quarterly goals, and yearly goals. Every year since I was 20 years old, I grab a Post-It and write about 5-6 goals on January 1st. Every so often, I open up my drawer to read it. If I reached a goal, I cross it off and keep striving for all the others. Are you ready to jump into the deep end while I teach you how to swim? When you purchase my eCourse, you get to book a one-on-one meeting with either me or one of my senior team members to talk about anything you'd like: questions, advice, interview to join Techees, tips on how to start your own recruiting agency, etc.

My eCourse can and will teach you everything you need to know about being the best recruiter. Tech recruiting is what I do, yet this course will teach you how to be a recruiter for any industry you choose.

I train people in hopes they will be better than I am. I give them everything I have. Why? Because there's plenty to go around and seeing people I have trained succeed is one of the best feelings in the world. **I'll teach you how to be the best and maximize your income.** You'll learn how to set yourself apart from the competition.

I got into this for the money (and lots of it), and likely you will too. But don't forget one thing…

You might start out in this for the money but it's the life-changing jobs you'll find for people; the companies that become successful because of your brilliant placement; all the good you'll do because you're no longer scraping by financially... those are the things that will really help you sleep with a smile on your face. Well, those and the $500 Egyptian cotton sheets you sleep on.

Congratulations on taking the first step by reading this book. Now it's time to take the next step. Start my eCourse today. This is your time. You decide and direct your destiny. And I expect to see a photo of you with your first big, fat commission check very soon!

Your Success Partner in Crime,
Brianna Rooney

Visit **www.BriannaRooney.com** to find out more and start the eCourse that will change your life forever.

Email **Brianna@techees.com** and connect on Linkedin. **https://www.linkedin.com/in/bmarie/**

Follow us on:
Instagram millionaire_recruiter

Twitter @BriannaRooney84

Facebook @millionairerecruiter

This Book and eCourse wouldn't be possible without so many others...

The hard work and dedication of my two favorite success partners in crime: Emily Stellick and Ben Markowitz. I am truly thankful for all you both do. I look forward to reaching that billion together!

My husband, Luis, and my two amazing little ones, Diego and Lima. Luis, I appreciate you for the passionate man you are. You are an incredible husband and father that is constantly cheering me on and keeping me in check. And Diego and Lima... my drive, my motivation, and my want for more are all only stronger now that I have you two. I love you more each day. I hope that you will be proud of what I've built and what I want to continue to build.

My mom, my dad, and, Blake, my stepdad. "Thank you" doesn't say enough. Without each of you, I wouldn't know what hard work and constant sacrifice looked like. You inspired me at such a young age, taught me to take care of myself, and made me understand how important money is.

Thank you and my love to you all!

Brianna

And now... if you want to be even more awesome like I did, and need help not related to recruiting. Contact these people who have helped me so much with this project:

Andrew Palosi at AdLeverage.tv. They are the best team. They filmed the eCourse, made our site, and so much more.

Josh Elledge and Rachel Underhill at UpMyInfluence.com. They taught me how to get my word out there. I've even been featured in numerous publications, including Forbes! Rachel is really the best and I enjoy working with her.

www.ingramcontent.com/pod-product-compliance
Lightning Source LLC
Chambersburg PA
CBHW071240220526
45468CB00002B/937